Mary's Three Gifts to Her Beloved Priests

Mary's Three Gifts to Her Beloved Priests

by
Rev. Albert Joseph Mary Shamon

Queenship
PUBLISHING COMPANY
P.O Box 42028 Santa Barbara, CA 93140-2028
(800) 647-9882 • (805) 957-4893 • Fax: (805) 957-1631

© 1997 Queenship Publishing

Library of Congress #: 97-067583

Published by:
    Queenship Publishing
    P.O. Box 42028
    Santa Barbara, CA 93140-2028
    (800) 647-9882 • (805) 957-4893 • Fax: (805) 957-1631

Printed in the United States of America

ISBN: 1-57918-005-1

Contents

Preface vii

Introduction ix

Chapter 1 - Priests, Mary's Beloved Sons 1

Chapter 2 - Mary's Priests and Satan's Strategy 7

Chapter 3 - Mary's First Gift: Her Book 13

Chapter 4 - Mary's Second Gift: The Marian

    Movement of Priests 19

Chapter 5 - Mary's Third Gift: A Second Pentecost.. 23

Appendix 27

Preface

Since 1973 Our Lady has been giving inner locutions to Fr. Stefano Gobbi, a priest from Dongo, Italy, just north of Milan, in an effort to prepare her priests and indeed all mankind for the very near-term occurrence of the climactic events recorded in St. John's *Book of Revelations*. These locutions have been published yearly in many languages in an always-expanding book entitled *To the Priests, Our Lady's Beloved Sons.*

In this short booklet, Fr. Shamon has done a marvelous job of encapsulating the essentials of what Our Lady is saying in that book: her formation of the Marian Movement of Priests; her request for regular attendance at cenacles of prayer by priests, religious and/or lay faithful; the consecration of all to her Immaculate Heart; and a trustful surrender to her urgings to each of us to live that consecration in a spirit of humility and littleness which she promises will lead us to holiness.

Fr. Shamon's booklet will encourage those who are unfamiliar or perhaps a little concerned about some of the content of Our Lady's book, which has the blessing of the Church, to enthusiastically embrace her call to holiness through trust in our Heavenly Mother. This booklet points out that the end result of priests and the lay faithful following the lead of Our Lady will be her greatest gift to all mankind, a Second Pentecost, through which the Holy Spirit will cause the renewal of the face of the earth and conversion of all mankind.

A copy of the latest version of Our Lady's book *To the Priests, Our Lady's Beloved Sons,* can be obtained by writing, calling, or going on-line to:

>The Marian Movement of Priests
>Rev. Albert G. Roux
>P.O. Box 8
>St. Francis, Maine 04774-0008
>Telephone: (207) 398-3375
>Web site address: <http://www.sjv.net/mmp/>

>In Mary's Name,

>Fr. Albert G. Roux
>Director (USA)
>The Marian Movement of Priests

Introduction

Not too long ago a woman from Rochester, New York, phoned me. She said: "Father, I've read so many of your booklets. You write clearly, forcefully and soundly, would you do us a favor? Would you write a simple little booklet on the Marian Movement of Priests to encourage priests to join the Movement and to start it in their own parishes?" Then she went on to say, "We have a powerful prayer group here in Rochester. We'll all pray to Mary to move you and to help you do this."

Well, I can tell you those prayers were heard. Even though I have been busy as a beaver, somehow I found time to write the following little booklet.

So, my thanks to all who prayed to make this project possible.

May Mary bless this small endeavor to make her messages to Father Gobbi known, loved, and lived.

May 13, 1997

Chapter 1

Priests, Mary's Beloved Sons

One year I made my retreat in Malvern, Pennsylvania. One night during the retreat, I went to the chapel at about eleven o'clock to pray my last Rosary, the Glorious Mysteries. Well, on the wall behind the altar in the chapel is a vast painting of the coronation of the Mother of God. She is seated and standing above her is Jesus placing a crown on her head. Surrounding her and Jesus are a host of saints: Francis of Assisi, Mother Katherine Drexel, St. Frances Xavier Cabrini, Kateri Tekakwitha, Junipero Serra, and a host of others.

Well, when I came to the Fifth Glorious Mystery of the Rosary, The Coronation, I was studying the painting. As I prayed, I was thinking to myself, "Mary, when I get to heaven, I hope, I suppose I will be on the fringe of the crowd of saints and you won't even notice me."

I no sooner had formulated that thought, when I felt as though Mary slapped me on the wrist and in no uncertain terms said firmly, "Don't you know who you are? You're a priest, an *alter Christus*, another Christ, precious, special, as dear to me as my very own Son. And, like my Son, you will have a special place right next to me. Don't you ever forget that!" Wow!

When Father Gobbi submitted his book of locutions from the Mother of God to Rome for approval, the only thing Rome wanted was to change the title of the book from "Our Lady Speaks to Her Beloved Sons, the Priests" to this title: "To the Priests, Our Lady's Beloved Sons." That's what a priest is—a beloved son of Our Lady Mary, just as Jesus was.

Once an Anglican minister asked a Catholic priest in England, "What's the difference between an Anglican minister and a Catholic priest?"

The priest answered, "The difference is, I can say Mass and you can't. I can forgive sins and you can't."

That was really a poor answer, because one of the errors today regarding the priesthood is to do just that—namely, to reduce the priesthood to a mere function—Functionalism. What makes a priest different from an Anglican minister and any other minister of religion is not the priest's function.

The essence of the priesthood is not a function. In philosophy we have this saying, *"Actio sequitur esse"*— that is, function follows upon existence, presupposes it. In other words, to be able to function, you first have to exist. A hundred years ago, I couldn't preach, because a hundred years ago I didn't exist.

So it was with the Son of God made man. Before He could celebrate Mass at the Last Supper and on Calvary, before He could forgive sins on that first Easter Sunday

Priests, Mary's Beloved Sons

evening, He had first to exist as a man. In other words, there had to be an Incarnation before there could be a Redemption—the Son of God had to become man, the Word had to be made flesh, before He could suffer, die and rise from the dead.

Likewise, with the priest—the priest has to become first another Christ before He can function as Christ. And he becomes another Christ through the character of the Sacrament of Holy Orders. Just as at the Incarnation the Second Person of the Trinity became man to form Jesus Christ, so the character of Holy Orders takes a man and unites him to the Son of God—so closely, so intimately, that he becomes another Christ, able to act, as Vatican II said, *in persona Christi*, "in the person of Christ" (Decree on Ministry and Life of Priest, #2).

A priest, therefore, is a priest, not because of what he can do, but first and foremost because of what he is—another Christ.

When St. Francis of Assisi was out walking one day with a companion, they met a priest and saw his guardian angel. Francis genuflected to the priest, but simply nodded to the angel. Later, his companion asked him why he slighted the angel. Francis answered that he had not slighted the angel, but was paying proper respect to the dignity of the priesthood; for, he explained, the dignity of a priest is even higher than that of an angel.

In the Civil War, snipers used to sit in trees trying to pick off the officers, for without the officers it would be easy to conquer the army. So some of the chief targets of

Mary's Three Gifts to Her Beloved Priests

Satan today are priests—Mary's officers. If the devil can shoot down a single priest, that priest would bring at least five thousand souls with him to the enemy.

Regarding priests, the Mother of God said: "My Adversary ...is trying in every way to do you harm" (Message 26a, Nov. 14, 1973). "If you only knew how much Satan tempts and obstructs them, torments and discourages them" (Message 77o, Aug. 5,1975). Referring to priests Mary said: "...if you only knew, my son (Fr. Gobbi), how human they still are: attached to themselves, to pleasures, to the esteem of others, to the goods of this world, to their own way of looking at things. They still doubt me, my son; and they doubt you (Fr. Gobbi) and the mission that I myself have confided to you.

"Satan torments them, sifts them violently, seduces them with pride and greatly discourages them! He bites furiously at my heel; he hurls himself with rage at my little children; he knows that soon it will be the faithful priests, and I with them, who will crush his head forever" (Message 77f-g, Aug. 13, 1975).

On the last night of the year 1975, Mary said: "Satan is maneuvering more and more openly in my Church. He has now associated many of my priest-sons with himself, deluding them with the false mirage that Marxism proposes to all: exclusive interest in the poor; a Christianity engaged solely in building up of a more equitable human society; a Church which would be more evangelical and therefore disengaged from its hierarchical institutions!...this real apostasy on the part of so many of my priest-sons, will become...open rebellion" (Message 90h-i, Dec. 31, 1975).

Sounds like Liberation Theology, doesn't it? And like all those other religions that put the people and the community, above God, Church structure and the hierarchy?

With a heart-rending plea, the Mother of God asks her priests to come to her aid. "Help me, O sons!" she begs. "Help me, my beloved sons, to keep this world from falling into the abyss! Help me yet save many of my poor lost children" (Message 145c,h, Jan. 21,1978).

"Priests," Mary exhorts, "unite...about the Pope,...love him, pray for him, listen to him! Obey him in all things, even to wearing the ecclesiastical dress... Spread courageously the Gospel of Jesus, defend the truth, love the Church; help all to flee sin and to live in the grace and love of God" (Message 167l,m,p, Jan. 1, 1979).

Mary's Three Gifts to Her Beloved Priests

Chapter 2

Mary's Priests and Satan's Strategy

Satan not only has his focus on priests, but he seeks to subvert them in his subtle, clever, diabolical ways.

His first ploy is to sow **confusion** within the Church regarding dogma, liturgy, and discipline.

Many of the truths revealed by God are mysteries; for instance, the Trinity, the Incarnation, the Real Presence of the Risen Christ in the Holy Eucharist. It requires humility to accept the mysteries of faith. But Lucifer is proud and he shares his pride with a few priests. He seduces them with vainglory and intellectual pride. He especially strives to get these priests to try to penetrate and understand everything of the faith, even the mysteries. The next step is to get them to reject any truth, no matter how reasonable, that cannot be understood by human reason.

The motive behind all this is the illusion of making the faith, mysteries and all, acceptable to all. So truth is corrupted with error. Truths are denied or they are spoken of in such an equivocal manner that confusion results—the smoke of Satan.

Mary's Three Gifts to Her Beloved Priests

Mary pleads with her priest-sons to defeat this darkness of confusion by the light of truth. She wishes her priests to live the Gospel, to proclaim it with strength and courage, in harmony with the Magisterium of the Church (Message 168, Jan. 28, 1979).

As anyone knows, the fruit of pride is rebellion. Was not that Lucifer's sin, rebellion against God? So the second ploy Satan uses to ensnare unwary priests is **rebellion** against the Church of God and her laws.

A priest has obligations: to pray, to give good example, to lead a holy and apostolic life. Yet, Satan has lured some priests into letting activity crowd out prayer: their Office, meditation, the Rosary, and even to hurry through the Mass without reverence or devotion. Thus they become defenseless when confronted with the powers of darkness. They become worldly, share its values, and end up proclaiming the world, and not the Word, to the scandal of the faithful.

From this worldliness springs a growing rebellion against canonical norms like celibacy or the wearing of ecclesiastical garb; rebellion against liturgical regulations, even to the point of introducing one's own personal tastes and whims in the celebration of the Mass.

Mary asks us priests to become like little children, and to let her carry us in her arms; and she will make us perfectly docile to Holy Mother Church.

But intellectual pride is a frightful thing; it is not content to sow confusion and rebellion among priests, it seeks to create **dissension** within the ranks of the Church. Satan's strategy is to divide and conquer. Satan is hate.

Mary's Priests and Satan's Strategy

Hatred is divisive. By dissension Satan foolishly hopes to crush the Church.

In centuries gone by, divisions occurred in the Church. But these divisions led to separation from the Church. So one could easily determine what was Catholic and what was not. But now, Satan has changed his strategy. He is fomenting divisions **within** the Church herself: pitting priest against priest, bishop against bishop, and cardinal against cardinal. I remember a dissenting priest telling me, "We're not going to make the mistake of the Reformers in the sixteenth century. They left the Church. We are going to stay in the Church and change her from within."

The great mark of the Church is unity. Unity is the will of God. "I pray that they may be one," Jesus said after the Last Supper. The bond of unity is love. The source of love is Holy Communion and the Holy Spirit—the sacramental grace of every Mass. "May all of us who receive the body and blood of Christ be brought together in unity by the Holy Spirit" (Eucharistic Prayer II).

There are two ways to tear down a building. One would be to start with the roof and work downwards. But this is a long, slow and tedious process. The other way is to put dynamite under the foundation and in one blast bring the entire building down. This is Satan's strategy now. He is goading a few priests, foolish enough to listen to him, to strike at the rock foundation of the Church, to dissent publicly from the Vicar of Christ on earth, Pope John Paul II. Yet Mary has singled out this Pope in particular as her son, especially loved by her and guided by herself (Message

170, Feb. 11, 1979). She tells her priests to unite themselves to him, to support him with prayer, to defend him and to follow him (Message 162, Oct. 17, 1978).

Yet a very few priests, blinded by intellectual pride, do rebel openly against the Pope. Others do so more subtly and dangerously. Outwardly, they will proclaim unity with the Pope, but inwardly, in their hearts, they will disagree with him and let his teachings fall into a void and in practice do the very opposite of what he teaches.

Mary called this the Eleventh Station of the Cross for the Church. This disobedience, this rebellion, nails the Church to the cross (Message 170, Feb. 11, 1979). We may wonder why the Church in one generation is more effective in evangelizing than in another generation. Well, as an example, consider the headlights of a car. When the glass is clear, the light sheds its beam far and wide; but if mud is spattered on the glass, the beam of light will be seen less and less. So with the Church, when her priests and children are holy, her radiating power for good and the spread of the Gospel are great; but let her priests and children sin, and continue to sin, and little by little the radiating power of the Church for good is greatly diminished—her vitality is sapped and affected.

Hell has two gates: error and persecution. Satan and his proud minions try to tear the Church down by sowing error within her; when that fails, they try to overcome her by persecution. So, the final ploy of Satan is persecution.

Satan persecutes the Church from without especially by Freemasons and Secular Humanists. Both of these

Mary's Priests and Satan's Strategy

groups are seeking to build a new tower of Babel; namely a city without God. Secularism preaches that this world is everything; this world is all that matters. Humanism teaches that man is the center of the universe; he is all that matters.

These builders are shrewd. They pay lip service to the Church to get her members to compromise, to go along just to get along. But through the media, the press, the television, they incessantly attack Christian morals and values and peddle, promote and praise the earthy, carnal, material values of the secular city.

G.K. Chesterton foresaw this danger in his classic poem *The Ballad of the White Horse*. In this poem, King Alfred, after having conquered and converted the Dane Guthrum to the Catholic faith, and having secured peace in England, sits and ponders on the future. Through Alfred, Chesterton warns of the danger that will threaten the twentieth century.

> They shall not come with warships,
>   They shall not waste with brands,
> But books be all their eating,
>   And ink be on their hands.
>
> They shall come mild as a monkish clerk,
>   With many a scroll and pen;
> And backward shall ye turn and gaze,
> Desiring one of Alfred's days,
>   When pagans still were men.

Mary's Three Gifts to Her Beloved Priests

How right Chesterton was—the threat to our civilization would not come from invasions by barbarians, but from bad ideas! The battle of the twentieth century would be ideological. How true! Who has reduced America to a secular city? Not barbarians, but men robed in black, sitting on the benches of the courts of the land, mild as monks, bookish and so-called learned. For who has robbed the land of God, of prayer, defended hard-core pornography, abortion, etc., but judges by raw judicial power.

Yet even this onslaught would be turned back were the Church not persecuted from within, by some of her own children, her beloved priests. Some, like Judas, betray her; others, like the other apostles, fall asleep and abandon her. This is her Gethsemane.

Yet all these trials are but the means whereby the Church is being purified. From the winter of these trials, the Church will emerge purer, more humble, more holy, more enlightened, stronger than ever. After winter comes spring! Then the words of the prophet Isaiah shall be fulfilled: "The desert and the parched land will exult; the steppe will rejoice and bloom. They will bloom with abundant flowers, and rejoice with joyful song" (Is 35: 1-2).

To assist priests to help conquer the powers of hell, to crush the serpent's head, and to usher in the springtime to the Church, Mary is giving her priests three gifts: a Book; her Marian Movement of Priests; and a Second Pentecost.

Chapter 3

Mary's First Gift: Her Book

Mary's first gift to her priests is a book, *To the Priests, Our Lady's Beloved Sons*, a book currently containing five hundred eighty-six "interior locutions" made to Fr. Stefano Gobbi since 1973. Fr. Gobbi belongs to the Company of St. Paul, a secular institute founded by Cardinal Ferrari. In the past, Fr. Gobbi has concelebrated Mass every year with Pope John Paul II in his private chapel and has his blessing.

The book containing the interior locutions to Fr. Gobbi has been approved by the Church. It is a "handbook" on how to live one's consecration to the Immaculate Heart of Mary on a day-to-day basis. If priests will read this book, they will know Mary's total plan "in its preparation, in its sorrowful actualization, and in its luminous and victorious completion" (Message 284i, Jan. 28, 1984).

About her book, Mary said this to her priests: "Read it...meditate on it, live it! Have no doubt; I am speaking to you" (Message 284j, Jan. 28, 1984). In that same message she says that we speak from our earthly experiences whereas she speaks from her heavenly experience—she speaks to us in the light of paradise. She sees no difference between all of her children, be they in heaven or in purgatory or on earth. This is why she is so close to us; and so are all the brother priests with her up in heaven. At her command they live and work with her for us.

This book is Mary's because it simply records the messages given by her to her little son, Don Stefano Gobbi. The saints in heaven can communicate in many ways with us on earth. God may give a message by locutions or visions or apparitions. The messages in Mary's book were given to Fr. Gobbi by divine locutions.

A locution is simply a message given from God or Mary in one of two ways: exteriorly or interiorly.

An exterior locution is **auricular**: the message is given by the sound of a voice and is heard by the ear. Remember the call of Samuel. When he was asleep one night in the temple where the Ark of God was, God called to him four times. The voice of the Lord sounded like a human voice, for Samuel mistook the voice for the voice of Eli—he thought that Eli had called him (1 Samuel 3:4ff). The same voice of the Lord had been heard often before, by Adam in the Garden of Eden, by Cain after he had killed his brother Abel, by the patriarchs and prophets of old, until the fullness of time when God spoke to us through His Son. On the road to Damascus, Saul was converted by a voice. "The men who were traveling with him...heard the voice but could see no one" (Acts 9:4,7).

The most common form of divine locutions, however, are interior. They are received either in the imagination or in the intellect.

Mary's First Gift: Her Book

Imaginative locutions happen in dreams. "The angel of the Lord appeared to Joseph in a dream and said, 'Rise and take the child and his mother and flee to Egypt'" (Matthew 2:13). In this way God spoke to Jacob's son Joseph in Egypt about the Pharaoh's dream (Genesis 40:8; 41:16ff).

Intellectual locutions are the infusion of new ideas directly into the intellect or the illumination of ideas already acquired, but in such a way that something new is learned. That's how the Holy Spirit spoke to the apostles on the first Pentecost.

An intellectual locution is soundless. Yet the message is so clear, so strong it burns itself into the soul so that it cannot be forgotten, even over the years. The message is so full of meaning that it instructs without loss of time. The message causes a great calm, peace, and joy in the soul. Finally, the message is operative: it accomplishes what it says. Thus on the first Pentecost, Peter fearlessly stood up before the people and spoke with the wisdom of the most learned men of his day (Acts 2:14). The Word acted on them as God did in the beginning, when by a word He created the world.

The locutions which comprise Mary's book to her priests are intellectual. Don Stefano writes them in a completely normal way, neither in a trance nor in ecstasy. He writes without interruption and without mental fatigue, without re-thinking or correction. He doesn't even do the thinking! Like the apostles on Pentecost, he simply knows, he understands, and he acts.

Mary told Fr. Gobbi, "...entrust yourself to me... Let it be I who build—moment by moment—your future. It is enough for you to say just as a little child: 'Mother, I trust you, I let myself be led by you. Tell me: what must I do?'" (Message 6a,c, July 21,1973).

Mary's first command to Fr. Gobbi was, "Gather together in a booklet whatever I have told you... And this booklet is to be disseminated as quickly as possible among priests; it will be the means through which I will bring them together from all sides and with which I will form my invincible army" (Message 15c-d, August 29,1973).

To tell whether a locution is from God or from autosuggestion or even from the devil, one need only judge its fruits. The locutions of Fr. Gobbi, Mary's book, give peace, and inspire humility and confidence in God. They detach one from sin and move one to do good. The messages are in complete harmony with Divine Revelation and the Magisterium of the Church. Already, Mary's book, the divine locutions to Fr. Gobbi, has touched the souls and hearts of tens of thousands of priests, many of whom were in situations of crisis; and it has moved the faithful to do much good. A good tree cannot bear bad fruit.

In her January 21, 1984, locution to Fr. Gobbi (Message 282), Mary remarked about the opposition her book had encountered; yet she said that it had done great good in every part of the world. Then Mary went on to answer two questions.

First, how should this book be read?

Mary said it must be read with the simplicity of a child listening to its mother. The child doesn't question its mother. The child just listens and does whatever she says,

Mary's First Gift: Her Book

because he knows she is his mother and she loves him and would never harm him.

Secondly, Mary asked, "What do I say of this book of mine?"

She says that it traces out the road she wants us to travel. It is a simple road, but a difficult one. Yet we must travel it for she is telling us the very things Jesus told us in the Gospel. She says that she is calling us to prayer, penance, mortification, to the practice of virtue, especially trust, hope and charity. Don't delay. Like a mother, she is telling us that grave evils lie ahead for us, but we can prevent them by our prayers and reparative penance. Therefore, with the courage of martyrs and the ardor of the apostles, live the Gospel to the letter!

Mary's Three Gifts to Her Beloved Priests

Chapter 4

Mary's Second Gift:
The Marian Movement of Priests

On May 8, 1972, while Fr. Gobbi was praying for fallen away priests at the little Chapel of Apparition at Fatima, the Mother of God made it clear to him that, through him, she would gather priests together from all over the world. By consecrating themselves to her, by being firmly united to the Holy Father, and by laboring to bring all the faithful to her, a powerful army would be formed. Under her banner, this army would resist the powers of evil throughout the world and bring the world to the feet of Her Divine Son.

The Marian Movement of Priests was her gift to her priests, to the Church. When a child is afraid, it runs to its mother; but when the child is in danger, the mother runs to it. These are times of grave danger, so the Mother of God, our Mother too, runs to us, her children—first and foremost to her beloved sons, her priests, to assist them. Her Movement is a sign of her perennial presence and of her maternal protection.

Mary's Three Gifts to Her Beloved Priests

She insisted that the Movement was her work alone (Message 284, Jan. 28, 1984). She said that was why she chose Fr. Gobbi: "My son, I have chosen you because you are the least apt instrument; thus no one will say that this is your work. The Marian Movement of Priests must be my work alone" (Message 5c-d, July 16,1973)

Mary wants her priests in her Movement to make three commitments: first, to be consecrated to herself; secondly, to be united with the Pope; and thirdly, to lead the faithful to herself. The weapon she has chosen to bring this about is the Cenacle of Prayer of the Marian Movement of Priests.

The Marian Movement of Priests is simply a replay of what happened after the Ascension of Our Lord. After His Ascension, the apostles gathered together with Mary in the Cenacle, the upper room where Jesus and His apostles ate the Last Supper. There they prayed for nine days. "All these (that is, the apostles) devoted themselves with one accord to prayer, together with some women, and Mary the Mother of Jesus, and his brothers" (Acts 1:14).

Following their nine days of prayer, the Holy Spirit came upon them and, through them, renewed the face of the earth.

I remember when I started the first Cenacle in Auburn, New York. We, priests and people, gathered before the Blessed Sacrament exposed. All during the Cenacle, Our Lady keep telling me that I was doing it all wrong. After our first Cenacle, I told my fellow priests about what Our Lady had told me. So we went back to Fr. Gobbi's book and we discovered that we were doing it all wrong.

Mary's Second Gift: The Marian Movement of Priests

A Cenacle is not a tryst with Jesus in the Blessed Sacrament. Rather it's a gathering of priests (the apostles) and/or the laity (the women and brothers of the Lord) around Mary, represented by her statue, for at least an hour of prayer regularly, perhaps once a week, to bring down the Holy Spirit upon the Church as on the first Pentecost and thus revitalize her and, through her, the world. A Marian Cenacle is to be a replay of what happened in the Cenacle after Our Lord's Ascension.

The Cenacle must not be a complex organization. Mary insists that it be "simple, spontaneous, quiet and fraternal" (Message 34e, Jan. 17, 1974). It is her work. She can do much with little, just as Jesus did with five loaves and with just twelve apostles. She demands that it be kept simple. All that is needed is a statue of Our Lady for her children to gather around to sing and pray. The heart of the Cenacle is the Rosary and meditation on her book, *To the Priests, Our Lady's Beloved Sons*.

Our Lady has asked that Cenacles be formed everywhere. Prayer, especially the Rosary, is the weapon needed today to crush the forces of evil. "Satan's pride," she promised, "will again be conquered by the humility of little ones, and the Red Dragon will find himself decisively humiliated and defeated when I bind him not by a great chain but by a very frail cord: the Holy Rosary" (Message 275h, Oct. 7, 1983).

In the Appendix is a format of our weekly Cenacle. The Marian Movement of Priests has other formats as well.

Mary's Three Gifts to Her Beloved Priests

Chapter 5

Mary's Third Gift: A Second Pentecost

The spirit of Mary's message is not one of "chastisement," but rather one of motherly love, reaching out in mercy and compassion to her children in order to comfort and help them in their sufferings, to heal the wounds of their souls, and to prepare them for the trials ahead.

Of course there is to be suffering ahead, we are in it now. But those sufferings are simply birth pangs, like the labor of a woman about to give birth to a child. Thus Mary said: "The great suffering which awaits you is to prepare you for the birth of the new era, which is coming upon the world" (Message 441j, Jan. 1, 1991).

What are we to do in these times of suffering? Mary said we are to live in her Immaculate Heart, for it is the refuge she herself has prepared for these times.

One thing she has warned against is not to project into the future. The future belongs to God. There is a "No Trespassing" sign on the future. To trespass is to have to pay the fine of fear and worry. Our Lady said: "I say to you, beloved sons, do not scrutinize the future; and thus neither anxiety nor discouragement will take hold of you! Live

Mary's Three Gifts to Her Beloved Priests

only in the present instant, in complete abandonment, close to my Immaculate Heart" (Message 81o, Sept. 15, 1975). Longfellow said the same thing in his *A Psalm of Life*.

> Trust no Future, howe'er pleasant!
> > Let the dead Past bury its dead!
> Act,—act in the living Present!
> > Heart within, and God o'erhead!

The Present is all that God has given us and all that He will hold us accountable for. Therefore, Longfellow concluded:

> Let us, then, be up and doing,
> > With a heart for any fate;
> Still achieving, still pursuing,
> > Learn to labor and to wait.

The message of Blessed Mary Faustina from the Sacred Heart was—Trust! "Jesus, I trust in you."

In the last decade of this century, we are entering into the time of the Triumph of the Immaculate Heart of Mary foretold at Fatima. The fruits of the Cenacles throughout the world will soon become visible. After the first Cenacle in the Upper Room in Jerusalem, the Holy Spirit came down upon the Church and within three centuries the pagan Roman Empire became Catholic.

Our Lady predicts a similar triumph in this decade. She says that we are now close to the Second Pentecost.

Mary's Third Gift: A Second Pentecost

"The Second Pentecost," she says, "will come like a river of grace and mercy which will purify the Church" (Message 428, June 28, 1990)—making it "a new Church for a new world, where my Son Jesus will reign at last!" (Message 10n, Aug. 1, 1973).

In this new era heaven and earth will meet in an encounter of love, light and life. We shall experience the Communion of Saints in a strong and visible way: we shall have close contact with the saints in heaven and the souls in purgatory. Could this not be the heavenly Jerusalem come down upon earth—the saints helping to transform the world into a new heaven and a new earth?

In this new heaven and new earth the Most Holy Trinity will be glorified: the Father will receive glory by His will being done on earth as it is in heaven; the Son will liberate mankind from the slavery of evil and sin; and the Holy Spirit will renew the face of the earth by enlightening minds to the truth and filling hearts with love. Satan will be defeated once and for all; he will be shut up in hell, never again to roam the world to harm it. Christ shall reign, and the Immaculate Heart of Mary shall triumph. God's kingdom will come on earth as it is in heaven (Cp., Message 453, Aug. 15, 1991).

To effect this Second Pentecost, Mary has asked us to pray this short prayer frequently:

"Come, Holy Spirit, come by means of the powerful intercession of the Immaculate Heart of Mary, your well-beloved Spouse (Messages 226k, June 7, 1981; 426a, June 3, 1990; 521b,n, May 22, 1994).

Mary's Three Gifts to Her Beloved Priests

In a word, to be consecrated to the Immaculate Heart of Mary means to pray, pray, as she directs, and to live the messages in her book *To the Priests, Our Lady's Beloved Sons*.

Appendix

Our Cenacle of the Marian Movement of Priests

1. Sign of the Cross.
2. Prayer
3. Hymn
4. Prayer
5. Rosary
6. Meditative reading—from *To the Priests, Our Lady's Beloved Sons*
7. Silence
8. Act of Consecration
9. Prayer for Holy Father
10. Concluding hymn

1. Sign of Cross.

2. Pardon Prayer taught by the Angel of Fatima:

   My God,/ I believe, I adore,/ I trust and I love you!/ I beg pardon for those/ who do not believe,/ do not adore,/ do not trust,/ and do not love you (3 times).

Mary's Three Gifts to Her Beloved Priests

3. Stand and sing the Lourdes Hymn: "Immaculate Mary"

   1. Immaculate Mary.
      Your glory proclaim.
      You reign now in splendor
      With Jesus our King.
      > Ave, Ave, Ave, Maria!
      > Ave, Ave, Ave, Maria!

   2. In heaven the blesed.
      Your glory proclaim.
      On earth we your children
      Invoke your sweet name.
      > Ave, Ave, Ave, Maria!
      > Ave, Ave, Ave, Maria!

   3. We pray for the Church.
      Our true Mother on earth.
      And beg you to watch
      O'er the land of our birth.
      > Ave, Ave, Ave, Maria!
      > Ave, Ave, Ave, Maria!

4. Kneel and pray the Angel's Prayer for the neglect of and ingratitude toward Jesus in the tabernacle:

   O most Holy Trinity,/ Father, Son, and Holy Spirit./ I adore Thee profoundly./ I offer Thee the most Precious Body and Blood, Soul and Divinity of Jesus

Appendix

Christ, present in all the tabernacles of the world,/ in reparation for the outrages, sacrileges and indifference by which He is offended.

By the infinite merits of the Sacred Heart of Jesus,/ and the Immaculate Heart of Mary,/ I beg the conversion of poor sinners. (3 times).

5. The Holy Rosary
Conclude by standing and singing the "Salve Regina."

Salve Regina, Mater misericordiae. Vita, Dulcedo, et spes nostra salve.

Ad te clamamus, exsules filii Hevae.

Ad te suspiramus, gementes et flentes in hac lacrimarum valle.

Eia ergo, advocata nostra, illos tuos misericordes oculos ad nos converte.

Et Jesum, benedictum fructum ventris tui, nobis post hoc exsilium ostende.

O clemens, O pia, O dulcis Virgo Maria.

V. Pray for us, O holy Mother of God.

R. That we may be made worthy of the promises of Christ.

LET US PRAY

O God, whose only begotten Son, by His life, death and resurrection has purchased for us the rewards of eternal life, grant, we beseech Thee, that meditating

Mary's Three Gifts to Her Beloved Priests

upon these mysteries in the most Holy Rosary of the Blessed Virgin Mary, we may imitate what they contain, and obtain what they promise, through the same Christ our Lord. Amen.

6. Opening prayer:

ALL: O Holy Spirit,/ whose work in the first Cenacle/ was to set on fire with zealous love for souls/ the hearts of all who were persevering in prayer with Mary,/ the Mother of Jesus,/ continue, we beseech Thee, that same work/ and draw into the Cenacle generous souls/ inflamed with the desire to labor therein/ for the greater glory of God and His Immaculate Mother.

Then have a meditative reading on one or more messages from the book *To the Prists, Our Lady's Beloved Sons*.

7. Silence for five or ten minutes.

8. Act of Consecration to the Immaculate Heart of Mary from Fr. Gobbi's book.

Virgin of Fatima,/ Mother of Mercy,/ Queen of Heaven and Earth,/ Refuge of Sinners,/ we who belong to the Marian Movement/ consecrate ourselves in a very special way/ to your Immaculate Heart.

Appendix

By this act of consecration/ we intend to live,/ with you and through you,/ all the obligations assumed by our baptismal consecration./ We further pledge to bring about in ourselves that interior conversion/ so urgently demanded by the Gospel,/ a conversion that will free us of every attachment to ourselves/ and to easy compromises with the world/ so that, like you,/ we may be available only to do always the will of the Father.

And as we resolve to entrust to you,/ O Mother most sweet and merciful,/ our life and vocation as Christians,/ that you may dispose of it according to your designs of salvation/ in this hour of decision that weighs upon the world,/ we pledge to live it according to your desires,/ especially as it pertains to a renewed spirit of prayer and penance,/ the fervent participation in the celebration of the Eucharist/ and in the works of the apostolate,/ the daily recitation of the holy rosary,/ and an austere manner of life in keeping with the Gospel,/ that shall be to all a good example/ of the observance of the law of God/ and the practice of the Christian virtues,/ especially that of purity.

We further promise you/ to be united with the Holy Father,/ with the hierarchy and with our priests,/ in order thus to set up a barrier/ to the growing confrontation/ directed against the Magisterium,/ that threatens the very foundation of the Church.

Under your protection,/ we want moreover to be apostles of this sorely needed unity/ of prayer and love for the Pope,/ on whom we invoke your special protection.

And lastly, insofar, as is possible,/ we promise to lead those souls with whom we come in contact/ to a renewed devotion to you.

Mindful that atheism has caused shipwreck in the faith/ to a great number of the faithful,/ that desecration has entered into the holy temple of God,/ and that evil and sin are spreading more and more throughout the world,/ we make so bold as to lift our eyes trustingly to you,/ O Mother of Jesus and our merciful and powerful Mother,/ and we invoke again today/ and await from you/ the salvation of all your children,/ O clement, O loving, O sweet Virgin Mary.

9. One Our Father, Hail Mary, and Glory Be...for the Holy Father.

    St. Joseph, Patron of the Universal Church, pray for us.

10. Stand and sing "The Fatima Ave."

    1. In Fatima's cove
       On the thirteenth of May,
       The Virgin Maria
       Appeared at midday

       Refrain:
       Ave, Ave, Ave, Maria!
       Ave, Ave, Ave, Maria!

Appendix

2. The Virgin Maria
   Surrounded by light,
   God's Mother is ours,
   For she gives us this sight. Refrain

3. To three shepherd children
   The Virgin then spoke
   A message so hopeful,
   With peace for all folk. Refrain

4. With sweet Mother's pleading
   She asked us to pray,
   Do penance, be modest,
   The rosary each day. Refrain

5. All Hail Virgin Mary!
   This star guides our way,
   Our country's protectress,
   America's Way! Refrain